THE PACIFIC NORTHWEST POETRY SERIES

Linda Bierds, General Editor

THE PACIFIC NORTHWEST POETRY SERIES

disquiet

POEMS *by* JOHN WITTE

University of Washington Press

Seattle & London

Disquiet, the fifteenth volume in the Pacific Northwest Poetry Series, is published with the generous support of Cynthia Lovelace Sears.

© 2015 by the University of Washington Press
Printed and bound in the US
Composed in Warnock, a typeface designed by Robert Slimbach
19 18 17 16 15   5 4 3 2 1

UNIVERSITY OF WASHINGTON PRESS
www.washington.edu/uwpress

Library of Congress Cataloging-in-Publication Data
Witte, John, 1948–
 [Poems. Selections]
 Disquiet : poems / by John Witte. — First edition.
    pages ; cm. — (The Pacific Northwest poetry series ; 15)
 ISBN 978-0-295-99451-2 (hardcover : acid-free paper)
 I. Title.
 PS3573.I917A6 2015
 811'.54—dc23

                                        2014034910

In memory of George Hitchcock
(1914–2010)

Contents

I. ilk

II. clay

III. kiln

I. ilk

KINGLET

A smoke-gray   snippet   flicking

mist   from the madrone   we had forgotten

it zipping   through the limbs   huddled inside

all winter   its brisk

swagger   ramping and sizzling   freaked

flashing its tiny   gold crown   as if to say

see how   in love we are   how brief

how fitfully   burning

FLEDGLING

I awoke   to singing
and clambered   out of my crib
over the dresser   to the small screened window
where I perched   birds flickering   around their nest
the hungry hatchlings   featherless   awkward I leaned
toward them   I cannot say where   I went flying
from the farmhouse   in upstate New York
I came to   in a white room   the broken face
of my mother   looking down   with wires
attached to me   a human child

HIS KITE

climbing higher   in his short life
there had never been anything   so brisk as this
creature   lashing its tail   and so he forgot
and ran toward it   toward what he loved
and the kite wobbled   as if confused
the gulls squealing   in memory
the beach   an emptiness   pulling apart
the boy he was   plunging   toward his kite
crumpled   what a moment ago   was reading
the invisible   hallways   and soft
walls of wind

PAPER PLANE

What a boy did
with a sheet   of paper being
lazy   not scrawl   his book report
or paint   muddling the colors   but carefully
fold it   like this   into a floating
eerily circling   almost
weightless   thing

THE ME

who raised the trumpet   to his lips

who learned breath   tongue   and double-tongue

in this way   escaping   who began to hear

ictus   cadence

and the me   who lifted stones

turning and   coaxing   his small grunts

at dusk   his blackened nail   his wall

trim   and true

but most of all   the me who swam

out across the lake   the waves swaying him

who gasped   who wrestled in the water   the wooded

island farther off   than he thought

SHIBA ONKO

Then the youngest   gazing

into a porcelain urn   astir with koi

fell in   and was trapped   his friends cried

and tore at their clothes   I'm telling this story

for you   Leo

swimming alone   at night

in the reservoir   one of the boys returned

with a stone   and hurled it   with all his strength

shattering the urn   the water broke   over him

and the dying boy   who cannot be

told apart   from the hero

lay gasping   saved

SARGE

Because we moved   into town
and there wasn't room   for such a big dog
because the boy   would not   understand because
so much   needed to change   because you led him
across the highway   because you yourself
were forsaken   as a child you
stroked him and said   stay here someone
will find you   and take care of you   because
you looked back   and he followed   you tumbling
under the wheels   because you lied   saying
he ran away   because   if he knew the boy
would never be   the same

PHANTOM

Rapt   fingers sticky

he connected   the fragile plastic

halves of the fuselage   squeezing on cement

attached the wings   and swept it   through the air

making the hectic   jet noise   in his throat

I see him   hunched

woozy from the glue   his plane

weightless   as a blown egg   he doesn't know

what it means   the ordnance   the napalm

canisters   tucked under the wings

like seed pods

JUST THIS TRAIN

ruckling past   flatcars

stacked with lumber   cattle cars

and rumbling gondolas of coal   the strobing

light between boxcars   between phrases   a drifter

in the doorway   not my father   traveling

town to town   looking for work

not a poem   we're not talking about

the engine crowding forward   its burden of memory

or the last car   trailing a streamer   of silence

just this   moving wall   this smell

of hot metal   the flickering

tons   the ground shaking

SATURN

Ringed   whorled

weird   the unexplored planet

of my childhood   what might have been

mistaken   for a sanctuary   was nothing

but galactic debris   loafers and bicycles

swept into your gravity   you may not

even exist   except as a sluggish

golden cloud   of gasses and gravel

O unknowable father   enormously orbiting

in the dark   you devoured the others

but I   the youngest   escaped

with my ghastly wound

THE ROACH

Remember how the world

flashed past   the dry swales

and canyons   the velour seats   we wrote on

with our fingers   arriving   at a dingy town

across the border   the place we finally

turned back   making it seem

like our destination   is that why

I remember it now   the little restaurant

the slowly paddling blades   of the ceiling fan

something falling   a roach   the size of a thumb

into your soup   it was hilarious   but you recoiled

in your chair   horrified   my older sister

and me living on   remembering

this   of all things

ORNITHOLOGY

An eerie bird   in the thicket

behind our house   you noted   its brilliant

face and breast   did it have   a cinnamon throat

perhaps a tanager   no you said   more of a turmoil

a blazing under   the black wing

did it fly   in buoyant

swoops   was its voice   a descending

sleepy warble   maybe a towhee   its eye burning

no you said   more an omen   an angel furtive

bird of my heart   you said   creature to me

NEST

Restless   the sparrow gathers

our hair   and lint   to line her nest

bits of foil   and plastic wrap   the cat's fur

and scattered downfeathers   she wants them

to know us   and not be afraid

tumbling out of their eggs   into a purse

of litter   beginning their life   of scrabbling

and swerving   at home in the world   making

their clear   wiry   rising calls

TOUCHING THE ANIMAL

Seeing you   the animal comes
closer   a darkness   heavy on its hooves
whiffling through   its wet nostrils
go ahead   touch it
but you're not so sure   what if it
turns on you   reaching out   your fingers
grazing   its warm fur   greasy and coarse
there   finally   you have touched it
not to kill it   this time
placing your hand   on its shoulder feeling
the animal   bolt   through your body

AUBADE

I'm awake   *what is it*
flickering   a wing   a woman's
breast grazing   my cheek   the wren's frenzied
chortling in the leaves   before we let go   of the dream
and dress   and crowd the highway   singing
here I am   singing   *what*
what   joyisit

THE BUMBLEBEE

doesn't listen   blundering

clumsily   through the blossoms   the words

devout   and disheveled   come to mind   its fur

pollen-dusted   it should not even   get off the ground

lacking sufficient amplitude   and lift coefficient   yet

doesn't it rise   like a hurt angel   its pronounced

gracelessness   fumbling the ovaries   woozily

stumbling   flower to flower

gathering the sweetness

MIND OVER MATTER

Witless   loopy with love
I began to believe   I could move
objects   with my mind   I would begin
with a light switch   then by sheer   concentration push
a matchbook   a tiny sailboat   across the table
I remembered little   of my prior life
now I dwelt   in the mysterious
house of my beloved   I would summon
all my strength   and heave   straining
until the switch   flipped   the current surging
through the wire   into the bulb where
the hairlike filament   seized
and began to glow

SNAILS

So that's why   we close our eyes

when we kiss   so the tongue

can work in the dark   the way it likes

so slick and nimble   no wonder the mouth

feels so empty   to the tongue   how it fills

with words slithering   and pushing   we cannot

get more naked   than this

our tongues touching   and sliding together

like snails   shooting their tiny

love-darts   our empty skulls

spiraling   behind us

CICADAS

What were they   chirring

in the breathless heat   and where

were they hiding   all around me   I was

six   and they shrilled   for a week then

fell silent   for seventeen years

a boyhood   passing as if

in a dream they returned   at twenty-three

their sexual buzz   and brittle coupling

their husks   clinging to trees then

they were gone   for so long

I forgot them   only the sleepy crickets

the languid summer days   seemed endless   but

there they were again   at forty   inescapable

countless   nowhere to be seen   ceaselessly

echoing   through my life

HEIRLOOM

Ours now   the lush thicket

the intricate family   rug I crept on

a baby   where a baby   now finds herself

bewildered among fruits   blooms   and branching

a peach repeating   the path   dwindling

in the foliage   its fertile pattern

imperceptible   from so close

PIE CASE

Cherry   coconut cream
key lime   we gaze   at the pies
circling   on their carousel   such sweetness
time conceives   a fly   landing
on the crust   the viscid
fillings congealed   the trays   revolving
like prayer wheels   or the chromosomal helix
like this poem   swiveling on its axis
a small motor   groaning beneath

MICROSCOPE

Enlarged   the letters decompose
the fly's wing   a fluted plate of ice
he leans into   his daughter's microscope
the unseen jewels   of sand   she put aside
wanting life   legible and fierce
but he is drawn   to the invisible   reading
on a blistered leaf   the hereafter   of molecules
the woozy   pollen-crusted   chasm of a flower
the eight eyes   and hairy   brazen carapace
of a spider   its mandibles
its magnified   glory

WIND

Was that me   my hand cupped

out the car window   catching the wind

was that when I learned   how nothing feels

like something   a river surging   the memory

of childhood spilling   into and out of

my hand   how something

a lifetime racing past   the swelling

of joy   and grief   feels

like nothing

II. clay

FLOATERS

There what   was that a face
at the edge of sight   or a scatter
of minnows   the eye's   tossed confetti
speaking of the body   falling apart   a clout
on the head   jarring loose   bits of cortical gel
like moths   or is it   the peripheral flicker
of memory   or is there   a world inside
this one   filled with ghosts

GOING THE DISTANCE

Starts out fast   light-footed   we love

the dance jab   and counter-jab   the stinging

flurry of punches   flinch and feint   the uppercut

clobbering   we learn about   the purpled

contusion   the blurt   the coming back

for more   gleet and sudor

the sounds   pummeled out of us

we see   how it will end   the room

tilting   the fearful   gazing around

the bleeding   unseen

IT SO

happens   this

being so   and so forth

so little time   so as to   feeling

so unsure   must it be so   broken up

febrile   freakish this   halting so

much so what   now it seems so

to speak so   help me

THEN ONE MORNING

he found everything   coated in dust
the teacup   the flowers   the surfaces velvety
with book dust   soot   scurf   he coughed the glittery
whorls moiled   he drew his finger through   writing
it wasn't always   like this   was it the dust
of sloughed flesh   or was it   the residue
of dreams   ghostly   wolf-gray
cloaking his world

LOVE AND LIFE

He coughs   you cough

you touch his hand   he gasps

in pain   and you gasp   love says

hold him   don't let him go   life says

it can't be helped   love says   follow him

into that   unknown life   says come back

do not go there   love says remember

how you ran   breathless

into his arms

GROCERY CART

Wheeling   the fretted
cagework   steely   sullen
wanting cheese and fruit   cans and dishsoap
our heave offerings   our child   strapped in
squirming   the chilled meat   cellophaned
unearthly   we yearn   our hunger
born again   we follow you
gleaming   pitiless

RIDDLE

       Not a stone   though hard

   not a calculator   beside the bed   not a clock

though it makes time   stop give us   another clue

not a book   not characters   you feel you know

   the twists and turns of plot   with its bluing

      its underbreath   not a crucifix

if that's what   you're thinking   a rigid agony

a rattling someone   trying the door   your finger

on the trigger   not a cellphone   a known voice

   echoing   in the chamber   not an apple

   though its seeds   cluster at the core

CESIUM-137

Returning in memory
from the hospital dump   the peddler
heaved the canister   onto his porch   and prized it
open what   was it a lump   of wax inside
glowing warm   the neighbors passed it
hand to hand   the children
rubbed it   on their bodies   not the ocean's
phosphorescence   breaking over them   leaving them
spangled   this was different   deeper   in delirious
memory wrestling the lead egg   into his wheelbarrow
staggering forward   yanked
this way   and that

FROGMAN

I awoke muddled

adrift all morning   at my desk

gazing into the screen   the sky   darkened

then rain   streamed the window   and I remembered

I was at an aquarium   undulant eels   and octopuses

ghosting past   a frogman   floating among them

his face   barely visible   behind his mask

dragging his squeegee   across the glass

WHAT BEGAN

as a day   at the beach

everyone there   in the dream   chips and pop

ska on the boombox   loosening our limbs   beginning

to sway   the kite waggling   the kids launching

their goofy   inflatable rafts   the dream

salami   the dream sand   warm underfoot

then darkening   the sky swelling

and crashing   ended

with bull-horns   life-boats pulling

everyone grasping   out of the water   but you

sister   gentlest of us   left

floating in the dream

SEIZURE

Instead of writing   I'm flying

to see you   terminal   entubed   passing

through clouds   instead of describing   my grief

I'm showing you   the man across the aisle

lurching in his seat   as if

buffeted by laughter   or sobbing

the steward holding him   so he doesn't beat

his face into the seat   in front of him   the turbulence

finally easing   he falls   into exhausted sleep

his breath   in gasps   instead of flying

the plane slows   nosing down

FIREFLIES

Flying home   I see you
in my dream   stricken   dimmed
flustered   by fireflies   you smile
grimace   and smile   sending a message
too ephemeral   to grasp   what was
familiar then   their on off
seems distant now   exotic   like angels
beckoning us   from the heaven   of childhood
they cannot cross   over the mountains   but hover
in memory   where our bodies   gleam with longing
and love   the light blinking   at the end
of our wing   our lives   so briefly
plunging   through the dark
the light   the dark

AT THE WAR MEMORIAL

No tears   at the memorial
for the war dead   the marble reflecting
our faces   did not move me   or the way
the black wall   engraved with their names
gradually receded   underground
but then I saw   how the letters crowded
and fell together   no longer names
but a silent   unraveling rain
streaming down

CROSSWORD

His walls bare   we found

his paper open   to the crossword

each square   inked in   down and across

intersecting   as if complete   yet not

a single   recognizable word

we could see   he was lost

for answers   or had he fallen back

into Polish   mangling the words   to fit

his first language   like a cryptic bird

a scattering of feathers   the body

pimpled   bluish

OXBLOOD

Returning to empty
his closet   his tired sheets
and dilapidated shoes   I remember
scraping the crusted   chemical scabs   and rubbing
the polish   his wing-tips   huge to me
heavyhearted   he reappeared
evenings   distant   indecipherable
I smelled   my darkened fingers   and he looked
down on his shoes   with satisfaction   the leather
shining   the scuffs   and acid welts
healed   I sent him forth
his shoes gleaming

GRAVITY

She falls   sweeping

his stone   face up   to the sky

so the mower   can pass over   the engraved letters

filling with   dirt and seeds   she cannot

stand   if only someone

would see her   at his bedside

she listened was he   still breathing then

he reached out   and pulled her

down   into his arms

THE WILL

No one dreamed   given the bloom
and clamor of your life   the toots and feuds
and sizzling poems   that you'd left   a will
your voice   solemn   the subsections precise
leaving us   the dented boat   the busted
mandolin   you trudged the mile
to the clinic   to beg them
to extend your benefits   grumbling
it seems like such a long way   gripped
your chest   and left   your papers scattered
your fly-tying workshop   aflutter with plumes
hurls and hackles   as if an exotic bird
had been   ripped apart

WHO KNEW

you were raised   evangelical

made to kneel   and pray   you taught

yourself to cook   and dabbled in fiction   dying

with a novel   in the drawer   the things you learn

at the service   who knew what happened   in the war

or that you hated nothing   more than the protagonist

with no mortal life   so when you introduced yours

he immediately left   to relieve himself

no relief for us   who return to work

and no more   life for you

who accepted us   as we were   less

than angels   our snits   and afflictions

our meager fellowship   and our audible

inevitable   trickling

THE WIDOWER

Where to begin   looking

through the window   in the dark   her face

framed   beside the bed   in the mirror

he found himself   unsure how to

go on   watching for her   under the ice

through the bone   the cut   the stained glass

she had never been   away this long   he thought

he saw her   on a passing bus   her head

thrown back   not shouting

but yawning

GRIEF

You chip   and nibble

the olive's   briny meat

guide it   with your tongue

between your teeth   scrape and

scuff the pit's   nubbly ridges

a thing   hard as stone

in your mouth

PUMICE

Over your face   in the photo

smiling on the beach   your teeth   bared

I place this   pebble   of pumice   yeasty

spumous   the stone floating   or blown

like sea foam   eased

of its weight

INSTEAD

I went to the pond

drawn by the dark   tons of water

and looked for a sign   of your passing

and though a thrush   lay splayed   in the grass

and the last light   drained from the sky   still

the birds choired   the minnows rose   dimpling

the surface   and the stars   appeared

it wasn't that   I'd forgotten you

and your funny mannerisms   but the world had

already moved on   its joy   undiminished

and the crow   a darkness   opening

its arms   and flying away

was only a crow

WHEN YOU COME TO LETHE

The sulks and slumps   the gray areas
you will put them   behind you   the off days
the eyesores   the vast   turgid sea   let them go
the oddments and omens   the stammering   the wraiths
and larvae   what are these   the slops and sludgy
waste stream   you will allow   these memories
to lapse   the radiance   the broken phrase
the smidgens   the fugitive   minutes
drink now   and forget

III. kiln

SONATA

My grandmother is buried
with others   in a common grave
in St. Louis   far from Poland   the place
unmarked   a jumble of ribs   and long bones
and muddy hair   I think of her   listening
to a sonata   the convergence of two
subjects   in different keys
Mozart   like her   lost to us
lowered into   a crowded pit   his wrist
and finger bones   that played   so exquisitely
even as a child   confused with   the shattered hands
of others   who simply toiled   in a sweat shop
in the new world   the music   a heaven
a paupers' grave   where our bones
meet   and mingle

THE SURGEON AND THE POET

Entranced   the surgeon reads

his patient's poem   its unruly blooming

and lurid   coloration   the poet suffering

the usual symptoms   vomiting   ataxia

aphonia   he saws

and lifts his skullcap   the tumor

a gleaming   spongy network   bizarre

anaplastic   he cannot   tease out   and sever

the mortal   entanglement   he cannot

save the poet   and the poem

though blossoming   like an unutterably

beautiful flower   in his mind

cannot save him

SCABSONG

Say the knife   slips

and does it hurt   the stinging

incision   the blood gummy   a thickening

granulation   crusting over   say the words

platelets   and fibrils enmeshed   in a network

of thready structures   what is a poem   anyway

but the stuff exuded   by a wound   helping us

heal   the scab falling away   the flesh

rosy   tender   leaving on your hand

a faint inscription

APOLOGY TO MY LEFT HAND

Look at you   beginning

to twist   and stiffen   the thumb

scarred   the nail black   where the hammer

missed the saw   jumped its groove   you never

cringe   or tremble   unable

to hold a pen   you willingly serve

your lord   the right hand   building the barn

the basilica   you are bloodied   steadfast

holding the board   with the dumbstruck

tranquility   of a martyr

JESUS AND THE SPLINTER

Didn't it   pierce him
didn't he glare   at the cedar plank
didn't he   have the right to curse   wasn't he
only human   after all   bringing his hand
close to his face   didn't he
squeeze   the splinter rankling
the wound   didn't it   weep oozing
its ichor   didn't he mutter   Eloi
Eloi   it hurts

LINCOLN

It was hard   to be happy

just ask Lincoln   spattered by pigeons

then the vandals   stole his head   wrenching it

off his shoulders   so we hired   a local sculptor

but the new head   was too abstract   wrong

for his frock coat   his expression

darker than before   as if brooding

on the flag bagging   over the gas station

the Constitution   rolled in his hand   like a baton

waiting to be   passed off and   can't you see

his head is too large   making him seem

pitiful   standing in the park

like a lost child

LEAVING THE MUSEUM

Quickened by art   we notice
the wet daubs of light   a broken
limb big as your arm   on the museum lawn
after the prints   and the dazzlingly trashy assemblages
we notice it   dragged by the wind   out of the tree
after the frantic spatterings   and video loops
we see it   fallen among the leaves
behind the marquee

AFTER YOSHITOSHI

He's there   or is he

dressed in animal skins   the thief

following you   deep into the marsh   hearing

in the moonlight   your flute   his hand

on his sword   wind

lashing your sleeves   and sash

you loved   a dramatic effect   clouds

scudding   the torn   scraps of song

the bandit crouched   or is he

twisting as if   something   the music

he cannot steal   only silence

were crushing him

NAPOLEON'S BATH

Rising in a cloud   of steam

he notices   behind the serene face

of Mona Lisa   the delirious plunge   of valley

the crumpled hills   green from the damp   years hanging

over his tub   an unsettled drainage   no one there

to conquer   the ridges beyond

her gaze   and hazy smile

her fierce   repose   he sees

the wet gleam   on her cheek   the geologic

folds of her robe   and beyond   to the crumbling

horizon   the world   her world   its ampleness

her ampleness   he stands   a small man

naked   vanquished

SAINT-RÉMY ASYLUM

a dumb fury of work

We must stop   Monsieur Van Gogh

from painting   for awhile   the landscape

writhing his mind   deluged   by the churning

sky and purple   flowering of Provence   we know

he is once again suffering   episodes

squeezing the worm   of paint

into his mouth   the lethal yellow   smearing

his tongue   the cerulean sky   and violet irises

his face a hungry   pelagic green   his canvas

a seizure   of color he swallows   the umber

and viridian   the world's oily   unguent

entubed   his poison   his balm

O

Rapture   or zero
numerous   among the letters
where death is   renounced   by our gasp
of joy   or our joy   revoked
by the icy   cipher
where something   and nothing   contend
trapped in a circle   where the vowel
resounds   in our mouths

Y

This night   and no other
this cold   this memory   this darkness beyond
the station   these stars   this crunching of boots
on the platform   this woman   holding a child
the distant whistle   the gate   clanging
the child   arching his back
making   with his mother   a Y
this gasping   and shunting   these words
and none other   this train   arriving
this big   sad animal

ASK

Is that   all of it
is that why   you sound so herky-
jerky   is this how   the mind halts
and bolts   is there something   wrong
do you have a question   yes Johnny   why
this poem   bilateral   like a leaf or face
as if we were   part of nature   after all
and is there   anything more   love
for example   or is that it
is that what you're asking

after Tadeusz Różewicz

BURNING THE BOOK

The reader is tired   of her book
its many characters   its twists and turns
of plot   she feels a sadness   for the trees
cut and pulped   to make the paper   the writer
toiling at his desk   she lets it drop
into the fire   writhing
open as if   all it wanted
was to flower again   her face aglow
aghast   in booklight   the gray petals
freckled with letters   the paper
collapsing into ash

GINKGO

My students look past me
into a ginkgo tree its leaves turning
yellower day by day sulfur to saffron
and apricot until today when the sun
broke through flooding the room with gold
like pollen on our faces and hands
on the open books there was nothing
I could teach them and nothing
more for them to learn

VESPERS

We'd also   like to know
why the birds   sing so   fervently
as the evening   starts to gather   is it
to locate one another   trilling and warbling
as if to say   don't be afraid   but if so
then why do they   sound so   joyful
their clear   piercing voices
singing   as the darkness
enshrouds them

WRESTLING THE ANGEL

Mstislav Rostropovich

And there   head bent struggled he
alone in the soaring   transept's half-light
wrapped the cello   in his arms   clasped
the neck scuffled   and grimaced   as if
thrashed by wings   the mike
live   recording
his huffs   and grunts
spending himself   in the surging
crescendo gasping   I will not   let you go
unless you bless me   and the angel   flummoxed
the day breaking asks   who are you   and there
blesses him   and if him   then us too
for a moment   listening
redeemed of all evil

THE SPIDER

luffing   in her web

not wistful   not dreaming this   dawn light

glinting the lattice   not brooding   or blissed

she listens   with her whole body   for the trembling

telegraphy   of an entangled fly   she is not happy

but neither is she troubled   least of all

silently   singing

her web torn   by my passing

she is not downcast   she does not hate

or love her life   but sets to work   remaking it

out of herself   not a mandala   she is not at peace

at the center   she is not asleep   or enchanted

not enthroned   she is   something

what shall we   call it

BUTTERFLY

Here my thinking

comes to an end   a clod of flesh

awakens   weightless   drying its wings

uncurling the long tube   of its tongue probing

the sweet recesses   of a lily   have I made my life

a willing instrument   tumbling end   over end over

the garden wobbly   with gladness   or terror

have I   let the wind   pitch

and convey me

Acknowledgments

My thanks to the editors of the following publications, where these poems originally appeared:

Agni: "Burning the Book," "Floaters," "It So"
Antioch Review: "Shiba Onko"
Iowa Review: "Jesus and the Splinter," "When You Come to Lethe," "Y"
Narrative Magazine: "Kinglet," "The Surgeon and the Poet," "Napoleon's Bath"
The New Yorker: "Snails"
Southern Review: "Mind Over Matter"

"Y" appeared in the anthology, *Long Journey: Contemporary Northwest Poets*, Oregon State University Press, 2006.
"When You Come to Lethe" and "Y" were included in *Discoveries: New Writing from the Iowa Review*, 2012.
"When You Come to Lethe" was reprinted in *What the River Brings*, Fae Press, 2012.
Poetry Daily reprinted "Shiba Onko."

I am grateful to Deb Casey for guiding me through these poems, and for the solidarity of Valerie Trueblood and Rick Rapport, George Gessert, Karen Ford, John Gage and, not least, my editor, Linda Bierds.

"Kinglet" is for Deb, "Just This Train" is for Anna, and "The Spider" is for Josie.
"Sarge" is for my brother, Mike, and "Love and Life" is for Marjorie Simon.
"The Surgeon and the Poet" is for Rick Rapport, in memory of Richard Blessing.
"Fireflies" is in memory of my sister, Janet Poskas (1944–2013), "When You Come to Lethe" is in memory of my sister, Lois Dolcemaschio (1946–2001), and "Pumice" is in memory of Tevena Benedict (1950–2005).

About the Author

CARLA PERRY

Disquiet is John Witte's fourth book of poetry and his second book in the Pacific Northwest Poetry Series. His poems have appeared in the *The New Yorker, Paris Review, American Poetry Review*, and numerous anthologies. The recipient of two fellowships from the National Endowment for the Arts, he lives with his family in Eugene, Oregon, and teaches at the University of Oregon.

Visit the author's web site at

www.johnwittepoet.com